IS-247.a: Integrated Public Alert and Warning System (IPAWS)

By

Fema

10/31/2013

IS-247.a: Integrated Public Alert and Warning System (IPAWS)

Table of Contents:

Course Overview

The goal of this course is to provide authorized public safety officials with:

- Increased awareness of the benefits of using IPAWS for effective public warnings
- Skills to draft more appropriate, effective, and accessible warning messages
- Best practices in the effective use of Common Alerting Protocol (CAP) to reach all members of their communities

Lesson 1: Introduction to IPAWS

Lesson Overview

This lesson provides an overview of IPAWS, its operation and benefits.

Upon completion of this lesson, you should be able to:

- Define Integrated Public Alert and Warning System (IPAWS).
- Identify the benefits of using IPAWS for generating warnings.
- Describe IPAWS operation.

IPAWS Overview

The Integrated Public Alert and Warning System (IPAWS) is a comprehensive, coordinated, integrated system that can be used by authorized public officials to deliver effective alert messages to the American public.

IPAWS is the nation's next-generation infrastructure of alert and warning networks. IPAWS ensures the President can alert and warn the public under any condition. Additionally, IPAWS will provide Federal, State, territorial, tribal, and local warning authorities the capabilities to alert and warn their communities of all hazards impacting public safety and well-being via multiple communication pathways. FEMA is upgrading the alert and warning infrastructure so that no matter what the crisis, the public will receive life-saving information via at least one path.

IPAWS Architectural Diagram

IPAWS allows alerting authorities to write their own message using commercially available software that is compliant with open standards. The message is then delivered to the IPAWS Open Platform for Emergency Networks (OPEN) where it is authenticated, and then delivered simultaneously through multiple communications pathways reaching as many people as possible to save lives and protect property.

The graphic below summarizes IPAWS architecture. We will go over it in detail later in this lesson.

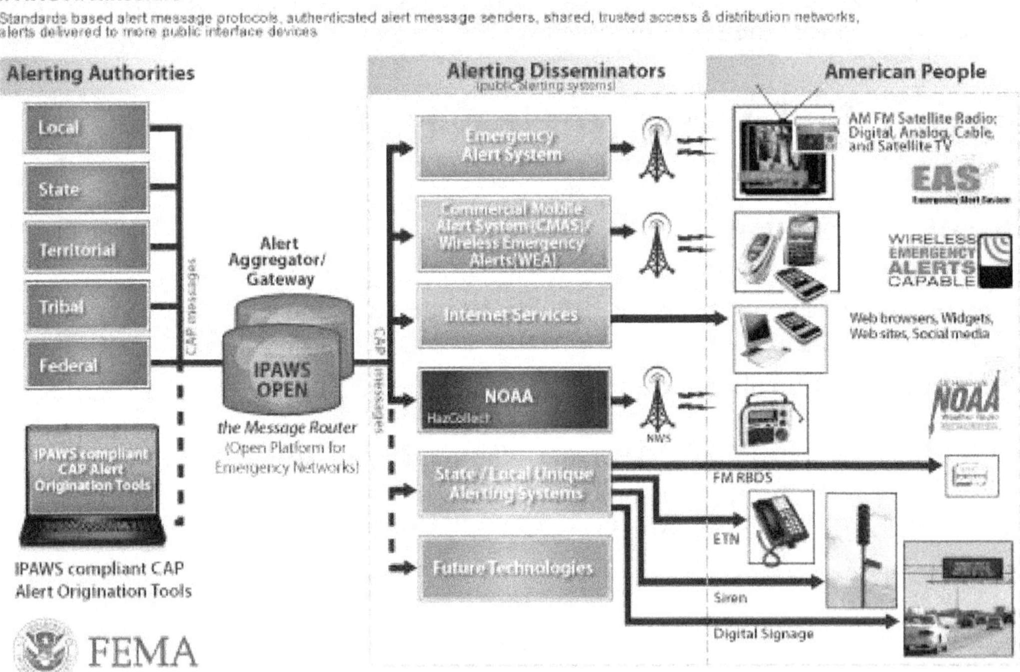

IPAWS Background

Click on each link below to learn more about the background on IPAWS.

- Presidential vs. Local Alerting: IPAWS ensures that under all conditions the President of the United States can alert and warn the American people in situations of war, terrorist attack, natural disaster, or other hazards to public safety and well-being. However, it also recognizes that most alerts and warnings are issued at the state and local level, allowing authorized users to create location-specific alerts that are scaled to cover areas as big as their entire jurisdiction or a much smaller area within their jurisdiction.
- Executive Order (E.O.) 13407: E.O. 13407 established as policy the requirement for the United States to have an effective, reliable, integrated, flexible, and comprehensive system to alert and warn the American people. FEMA is designated within the Department of Homeland Security (DHS) to implement the policy of the United States for a public alert and warning system as outlined in E.O. 13407 and has established a program office to implement IPAWS. FEMA and its federal partners, the Federal Communications Commission (FCC), the National Oceanic and Atmospheric Administration's (NOAA's) National Weather Service (NWS) and the DHS Science and Technology Directorate are working together to transform the national alert and warning system to enable rapid dissemination of authenticated alert information over as many communications channels as possible.
- FCC Orders: The FCC's role includes prescribing rules that establish technical standards for the Emergency Alert System (EAS), procedures for EAS participants to follow in the event the EAS is activated, EAS testing protocols, and approving state EAS plans. Additionally, the FCC issues rules establishing requirements for the Commercial Mobile Alert System.
- Common Alerting Protocol (CAP): The Common Alerting Protocol (CAP) is a simple, flexible data interchange format for collecting and distributing "all-hazard" safety notifications and emergency warnings over information networks and public alerting systems. CAP provides compatibility with all kinds of information and public alerting systems, including those designed for multilingual and access and functional needs populations. FEMA has adopted CAP and the IPAWS CAP Profile to ensure compatibility with the requirements of existing and emerging dissemination systems.

FEMA IPAWS Federal Partnerships

FEMA has partnered with recognized government and industry leaders and technical experts to ensure that the IPAWS program incorporates the latest technology and is practical for prospective users including local broadcasters, emergency responders and the general public. FEMA's partners in the development of the IPAWS program include:

- Federal Communications Commission (FCC): The FCC establishes the rules for broadcasters, cable system operators, and other participants regarding the technical requirements of the Emergency Alert System (EAS) and the rules for commercial mobile service providers who opt to participate in the voluntary Commercial Mobile Alert System.
- National Weather Service (NWS): The NWS provides emergency weather and tsunami information to alert the public of dangerous local weather conditions and other emergencies. Go to *http://alerts.weather.gov/* for more information on the NWS implementation of CAP.

IPAWS Benefits–One Input, Multiple Outputs

Do you recall the IPAWS architecture diagram reviewed earlier? Recall that IPAWS allows authorized alerting authorities to write their own message using commercial software that is compliant with OPEN standards. A message only has to be input once, and once authenticated; it is delivered over multiple communications pathways, including the Emergency Alert System, commercial mobile services, Internet services, NWS services, state and local alerting systems, and alerting technologies for persons with access and functional needs.

IPAWS Benefits–Geotargeted

IPAWS will ensure that the President can reach the American people, but it also recognizes that most alerts and warnings are issued at a state and local level. Alerting authorities can create location-specific alerts that are scaled to cover areas as big as their entire jurisdiction or a much smaller area within their jurisdiction, depending on the delivery capabilities of the system used for public dissemination.

For example, alerts relayed via EAS and broadcast by a local TV station will cover the entire viewing area of the station. Alerts relayed by CMAS are required to be delivered to an entire county although some cellular service providers may opt to broadcast to smaller affected areas.

IPAWS Benefits-Standardized Messaging Format

The Common Alerting Protocol (CAP) is an open, non-proprietary digital message format for all types of public and private emergency alerts and notifications, which can be delivered across multiple communications pathways such as:

- Broadcast TV and radio
- Cable and satellite TV and radio
- Mobile/cellular and wireless devices
- Signage
- Emerging technologies

You will learn more about CAP in *Lesson 3–Common Alerting Protocol Message Composition*.

IPAWS Benefits–Rich Content (Multimedia)

In addition to emergency alert-required data, CAP alerts delivered by IPAWS may carry rich information such as images, audio, video, geospatial data, etc., that alert originators may include and disseminators may utilize to provide supplemental information to their audiences.

The photo at the right is a picture of Amber Hagerman, for whom the national America's Missing: Broadcast Emergency Response (AMBER) alert system was named.

IPAWS Benefits–Reliability, Redundancy, Security and Accessibility

IPAWS uses redundant alerting paths (TV, radio, cell phone, etc.) to increase the chance an alert will reach the public. IPAWS hardware and software components are designed to be reliable. The digital signature capability ensures message integrity and authenticity. Finally, CAP provides compatibility with public alerting systems, including those designed for multilingual populations and those with access and functional needs.

IPAWS Architectural Diagram and Operation

Federal, State, territorial, tribal, and local warning/alerting authorities are in charge of alerting their communities of all hazards using IPAWS-compliant alert origination tools.

Alert origination tools are software products used by emergency managers, public safety officials, and other alerting authorities to create and send critical life saving messages to the public.

The centralized alert aggregator/gateway receives CAP alert messages from various message origination/authoring tools, authenticates the sender, and sends the alert messages to IPAWS-compliant dissemination systems.

Multiple alert dissemination systems will have access to IPAWS:

- IPAWS alerts can be delivered by the Emergency Alert System, using AM, FM, and satellite radio as well as broadcast, cable, and satellite TV. Equipment used by Emergency Alert System participants (broadcasters, cable TV operators, etc.) monitor IPAWS to retrieve CAP alerts intended for their geographic area. CAP is converted to legacy EAS format in accordance with manufacturer guidelines and is relayed to the public.
- Alerts can be delivered via the Commercial Mobile Alert System (CMAS) that allows customers who own a CMAS enabled mobile device to receive geographically targeted messages alerting them of imminent threats to safety in their area (including Presidential and AMBER alerts). Participating cellular mobile service providers receive and route IPAWS alerts to cell towers in the affected area. IPAWS is the sole means of accessing CMAS.
- The National Weather Service operates the All-Hazards Emergency Message Collection System (HazCollect) to deliver "Non-Weather Emergency Messages" (NWEMs) through NOAA Weather Radio and other NWS dissemination services. IPAWS is the sole automated system for routing alerts to HazCollect.
- Alerts will be available on the Internet through web based applications, email, instant messaging, social media, and RSS/ATOM feeds. Both public and private sector services may monitor IPAWS and disseminate alerts.
- State, local, territorial, and tribal alerting systems such as emergency telephone networks, sirens, and digital road signs may also be configured to retrieve alerts from IPAWS once they are IPAWS/CAP compliant.
- Finally, CAP and IPAWS make it possible to integrate future alerting technologies and systems.

Resources

- **FEMA IPAWS Website**: For more information on IPAWS, view the FEMA IPAWS website (*https://www.fema.gov/integrated-public-alert-warning-system*).
- **Executive Order (E.O.) 13407**: Complete text of E.O. 13407 is available at *http://edocket.access.gpo.gov/2006/pdf/06-5829.pdf*.
- **FCC Orders**: To access FCC EAS rules and regulations, go to *http://ecfr.gpoaccess.gov/cgi/t/text/text-idx?c=ecfr&sid=75127c72007aa6a3f1ce8fda8cb814e2&rgn=div5&view=text&node=47:1.0.1.1.11&idno=47*. For access to a list of state EAS contacts and plans go to *http://transition.fcc.gov/pshs/services/eas/chairs.html*.
- **CMAS**: go to *http://www.fema.gov/pdf/emergency/ipaws/cmas_factsheet.pdf* to learn more about CMAS.
- **FCC rules pertaining to CMAS:** *http://www.gpo.gov/fdsys/pkg/CFR-2010-title47-vol1/pdf/CFR-2010-title47-vol1-part10.pdf*
- **NOAA/NWS HazCollect System:** go to *http://www.weather.gov/os/hazcollect/* for further information about HazCollect.
- **OASIS Emergency Management Technical Committee:** go to *http://www.oasis-open.org/committees/tc_home.php?wg_abbrev=emergency* for further information about activities of OASIS relating to emergency management.
- **EAS-CAP Industry Group**: go to *http://www.eas-cap.org* to access the EAS-CAP Industry Group website.

Lesson Summary

This lesson provides an overview of IPAWS, its operation and benefits.

You should now be able to:

- Define Integrated Public Alert and Warning System (IPAWS)
- Identify the benefits of using IPAWS for generating warnings
- Describe IPAWS operation

In the next lesson, you will learn about and apply the criteria for creating appropriate, effective and accessible alert and warning messages.

Lesson 2: Appropriate, Effective, and Accessible Alert and Warning Messages

Lesson Overview

This lesson provides an overview of creating appropriate, effective, and accessible alert and warning messages.

Upon completion of this lesson, you should be able to:

- Identify the basis for determining who is authorized to send IPAWS alert and warning messages
- Apply criteria for sending appropriate alert messages
- Identify the components of effective alert and warning messages
- Apply criteria for creating accessible alert and warning messages
- Describe factors that influence public response to warning messages
- Discuss the myths associated with public response to warning messages

Who Can Send IPAWS Alerts and Warning Messages?

Designated Alerting Authorities at the Federal, State, Local, Tribal and Territorial levels are authorized to send alerts and warning messages to their respective communities. After successfully completing this course, Designated Alerting Authorities may apply to FEMA for access to IPAWS on behalf of their jurisdictions.

There are a number of government programs with written plans that may indicate specific alerting authorities, including:

- State/Regional/Local Emergency Alert System Plan
- State/Tribal/Local Emergency Operations Plan (Warning Annex)
- State/Regional/Local AMBER Alert Plan
- Radiological Emergency Preparedness Program Plan
- Chemical Stockpile Emergency Preparedness Program Plan
- Other hazard specific emergency plans or interjurisdictional agreements

Collaborative Operating Group (COG)

A Collaborative Operating Group (COG) is a term used by IPAWS to designate an organization that is responsible for coordinating emergency management/incident response activities and public alerting. It typically consists of public safety officials who need to coordinate actions, communicate and exchange information in a collaborative environment. Examples of organizations that may constitute a COG include state, regional, county, or municipal emergency management/incident response organization, state law enforcement agency, Federal agency, military unit, public health department, fire services organization, mutual aid partners, etc.

A COG is established when a sponsoring organization executes a Memorandum of Agreement (MOA) with FEMA. A Federal, State, territorial, or local organization (as defined by the Stafford Act *https://www.fema.gov/library/viewRecord.do?fromSearch=fromsearch&id=3564*), a federally recognized Native American Indian tribe, or other private nonprofit organizations eligible under the Public Assistance Program may apply for authentication.

Applying for Alerting Authority

In addition to executing an MOA, the COG must also apply for specific alerting authorities, including the geographic extent of authority (e.g. county) and types of alerts (event codes, e.g. CAE - Child Abduction Emergency, discussed later in this course).

Before submitting to FEMA, the application must be reviewed by a state authority to ensure that the request is consistent with state Emergency Alert System, AMBER, other emergency operations plans and current practice. Further details regarding the application process may be found on the IPAWS website (*https://www.fema.gov/integrated-public-alert-warning-system*).

Criteria for Issuing Warnings

Deciding whether to issue a public warning can be a difficult decision. Ultimately it will be a matter of local judgment; however, it will be helpful to have an outline of decision criteria to assist you with the process. When deciding whether to issue a public warning, the following criteria can be applied:

1. Does the hazardous situation require the public to take immediate action?
2. Does the hazardous situation pose a serious threat to life or property?
3. Is there a high degree of probability the hazard situation will occur?

Your State or Local EAS Plan or other emergency plans may provide criteria for issuing public alerts, including activating the Emergency Alert System, and if so, should be incorporated into your local procedures.

Application of Criteria for Appropriately Issuing Alert Messages

Your alert authoring software will provide fields that correspond to the previous three questions. Each field will provide a list of values to select from. In order to be routed to the Commercial Mobile Alert System, the alert must contain certain values for these fields, reflecting "Imminent Threat:"

1. Urgency: Immediate or Expected
2. Severity: Extreme or Severe
3. Certainty: Observed or Likely

Although not currently required, these values may also provide a good rule of thumb for relaying public alerts via the Emergency Alert System. An example of the application of these criteria by the National Weather Service for a Tornado Warning is shown in the adjacent graphic.

Alerting Criteria Derived from EAS Specific Area Message Encoding (SAME) Protocol

Assuming you are starting from an occurring or impending potentially hazardous event, the first question is whether or not the event meets the appropriate definitions for warning or emergency, as defined by the SAME protocol.

- Warning messages: These are issued for those events that alone pose a significant threat to public safety and/or property, probability of occurrence and location is high, and the onset time is relatively short.
- Emergency messages: These are issued for those events that by themselves would not kill or injure or do property damage but indirectly may cause other things to happen that result in a hazard.

Your State or Local EAS Plan or other emergency plans may provide criteria for issuing public alerts, including activating the Emergency Alert System, and if so, should be incorporated into your local procedures.

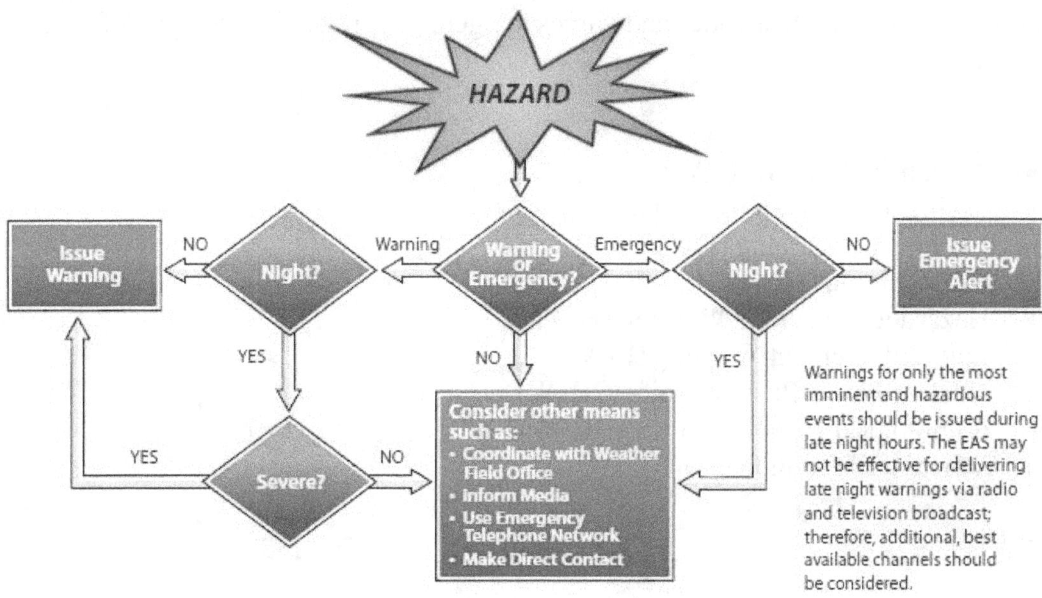

Appropriate Event Names and Event Codes

Now let us look at the various event names and codes used for disseminating warning messages. All three major public dissemination services–EAS, CMAS, and HazCollect– use the same hazardous event names and corresponding event codes that are derived from FCC rules.

The following factors should be considered in the selection of appropriate event codes. Click on each link below to learn more about the factors:

- Hazardous weather and coastal events: Event codes relating to hazardous weather and coastal events are reserved for the National Weather Service.
- State/Local Emergency Plans: State or local EAS plans may limit the types of codes which EAS participants (e.g., broadcasters) are assigned to monitor for EAS broadcast.
- Relevant hazards: Certain types of hazards may not be relevant to the risks in your community. For example, volcanoes or avalanches may not be present in your part of the country.
- Event codes specified in your application and implemented in IPAWS: The event codes that are specified in your application and implemented in IPAWS will determine which types of alerts are relayed to the dissemination services.
- Local knowledge: Finally, the selection of event code may determine what is displayed in a television "crawl" and your selection of event code may depend on what members of your community will understand based on local practice.

Appropriate Use of Hazard-specific Event Names/Codes

The following list of event codes and names are generally related to the type of hazardous situation:
Warnings:

- Avalanche Warning (AVW)
- Civil Danger Warning (CDW)
- Earthquake Warning (EQW)
- Fire Warning (FRW)
- Hazardous Materials Warning (HMW)
- Law Enforcement Warning (LEW)
- Nuclear Power Plant Warning (NUW)
- Radiological Hazard Warning (RHW)
- Volcano Warning (VOW)

Emergencies:

- Avalanche Watch (AVA)
- Child Abduction Emergency (CAE)

- Civil Emergency Message (CEM)
- Local Area Emergency (LAE)
- 911 Telephone Outage Emergency (TOE)

Appropriate Use of Instruction-specific Event Names/Codes

If you wish to focus more on the instructions to the public than the particular hazard, there are two instruction-specific event names/codes available:

- Evacuation Immediate (EVI): This event name/code is most appropriately used to instruct the public to evacuate for imminent events. For longer lead times, (e.g. several days), other methods of communication may be more appropriate such as media advisories.
- Shelter in Place Warning (SPW): This event name/code may be appropriate for hazardous materials, radiological, law enforcement, or other types of events; however it is more effective if your community has been educated as to its meaning in advance.

Components of Effective Warning Messages

Effective warnings are those that result in members of the public taking recommended actions to protect themselves. To help ensure that warning messages are effective, they must be issued in a timely manner and the following components should be included:

- Specific Hazard: What is/are the hazards that are threatening? What are the potential risks for the community?
- Location: Where will the impacts occur? Is the location described so those without local knowledge can understand their risk?
- Timeframes: When will it arrive at various locations? How long will the impacts last?
- Source of Warning: Who is issuing the warning? Is it an official source with public credibility?
- Magnitude: A description of the expected impact. How bad is it likely to get?
- Likelihood: The probability of occurrence of the impact.
- Protective Behavior: What protective actions should people take and when? If evacuation is called for, where should people go and what should they take with them?

Accessible Alert and Warning Messages

How you write an alert/warning message is nearly as important as what you write. Poorly written warnings can undermine both understanding and credibility.

"Style" refers to how you write. Here are some style elements to consider when writing accessible and usable alert and warning messages. Be:

- Specific: If the message is not specific enough about the "Who? What? When? Where? Why? How?," the public will spend more time seeking specific information to confirm the risk. If necessary, be specific about what is or is not known about the hazard.
- Consistent: An alert/warning should be internally consistent, that is, one part of the message should not contradict another part. It should be consistent with messages that are distributed via other channels. To the extent possible, alerts/warnings should be consistent from event to event, to the degree that the hazard is similar.
- Certain: Avoid conveying a sense of uncertainty, either in content or in tone. Confine the message to what is known, or if necessary, describe what is unknown in certain terms. Do not guess or speculate.
- Clear: Use common words that can easily be understood. Do not use technical terminology or jargon. If protective instructions are precautionary, state so clearly. If the probability of occurrence of the hazard event is less than 100%, try to convey in simple terms what the likelihood of occurrence is.
- Accurate: Do not overstate or understate the facts. Do not omit important information. Convey respect for the intelligence and judgment of your public.

Accessible Alert and Warning Messages for Persons with Access and Functional Needs

As the message originator, you should keep in mind the needs of persons with access and functional needs.

- Clear and simple language: A general guideline to follow is to use clear and simple language whenever possible, with minimal use of abbreviations. The most important information should be presented first.
- Text-to-speech conversion: Care must be taken in composing text that is converted to audio by text-to-speech equipment. Consult your NWS Weather Forecast Office for local guidance regarding NOAA Weather Radio requirements.
- Consistent audio: IPAWS and CAP can accommodate pre-recorded audio files that may be used by Emergency Alert System participants (e.g., broadcasters) and that assist the blind or those with low vision. The audio should be as consistent as possible with the text and should ensure that any abbreviations are spoken as full words.
- Ample text and audio to explain images/maps: Since IPAWS OPEN provides the capability to deliver multimedia messages, ample text and audio should be provided to explain images or maps, so that message recipients can understand the meaning of what is being conveyed graphically.
- Screen reading and text-to-speech devices: Some mobile devices and currently available software provide screen reading and text-to-speech conversion

capabilities for alerts delivered via Internet technologies. When considering these and other translation technologies, craft messages that avoid non-standard language formats and terminology.

Accessible Alert and Warning Messages for Persons with English as a Second Language

Non-English-speaking persons may not understand warnings that are provided in English. Communities with high percentages of non-English-speaking people should issue warnings in the primary language(s) of the population as well as in English.

IPAWS does not provide translation services, but it is capable of accepting and relaying alerts in multiple languages as composed by the alert originator.

Your alert authoring or other software programs may provide automated translation, but you should validate any automatically translated text with a speaker of the language to avoid errors. The use of pre-translated templates may serve to minimize the amount of information requiring translation for actual alerts.

Features of modern communication devices owned by end users can also provide translation of IPAWS alerts to the targeted language supported by the device.

Good and Bad Warning Message Example

Review each of the messages below and decide which a good and which a bad message is.

Message (A): 50 percent chance of dam failure. People in Ogdenville should consider evacuating.

Message (B): A dangerous wildfire is moving towards North Haverbrook and is expected to reach the north edge of town within the next hour. All persons remaining within the hazard area must evacuate now to a safe location to the west or east. A shelter is now open at Waverly Hills High School Gym. Pets are permitted.

Message (A) is an example of a bad message. It lacks certainty which may not motivate action. It does not give clear protective action by saying "consider evacuating" vs. "evacuate."

Message (B) is an example of a good message. It clearly states what the threat is, what area is threatened, and what specifically to do.

Best Practice Example—Using Planning Templates

The use of templates, tailored to those hazards likely in your warning area, can help prevent errors or omissions that can occur in moments of urgency. Using a template that incorporates pre-approved language can reduce delays in issuing alerts and warnings. Finally, if you need to use a language in addition to English, your templates can be translated in advance.

Your alert authoring software may provide the capability to create and reuse templates. If not, you can use word processing software to store your template and create your message to copy and paste into your alerting software. It is recommended that if you do utilize templates, customize them for the types of hazardous events that may occur in your area. The adjacent graphic shows an example of an evacuation warning template.

Sample Template

Disasterville Template for Emergency Alert System Message

Immediate Evacuation Order (EVI)

Replace all bracketed text below

(Headline field)

Immediate Evacuation Ordered for *[geographic description of area to be evacuated]*

(Description field)

Effective immediately, and extending until *[further notice or expiration time]*, the Mayor of Disasterville has issued an evacuation order for all persons living, working, or travelling in the vicinity of *[geographic description of area to be evacuated].* This area is at immediate risk from *[brief description of the hazardous conditions]*.

(Instruction field)

To protect yourself and your family from this dangerous situation, the following actions are strongly urged:

*Leave your home or workplace immediately for a safe destination outside the hazard area via *[specify recommended route(s) of travel]*.

*Take only pets and essential items such as medications with you.

*[*Instruction related to school children if applicable, e.g. Do not pick up your children from school. They are being evacuated by school officials.]*

A shelter operated by *[organization, e.g. the Red Cross]* is available at *[address of public shelter]*. If you need evacuation assistance, call 555-9999. Do not call 9 1 1 unless you have a serious personal emergency. For further information, tune to radio station KKKK.

Factors Influencing Public Response to a Warning

Accessibility of alert and warning messages refers to whether individuals hear and understand them. An appreciation of the multiple social factors that influence accessibility is useful. The primary response factors that influence the public's response to a warning are:

- Interpretation of message: When different people listen to the same message, there may be a variation in what they hear, leading to different interpretation and response.
- Previous experiences: Often people will rely on their previous experiences with the hazard to determine what actions they initially take (or don't take).
- Observations: Individual responses to warnings vary, but most people will seek some form of confirmation. For example, some people will look for more information through environmental cues, while others will seek to contact from other trusted sources. Optimism bias (thinking that "disasters happen to other people") is overcome with confirmation.
- Level of community interaction: People who have more contacts in the community will receive more warnings and are more likely to act; also, they are more likely to trust officials.
- Perception of risk/proximity: People tend to make a rapid assessment of the relative safety of their location, producing an emergent perception of risk. If their perception of personal risk is high, people will act quickly. When the perception is low, they will delay acting.
- Length of residency: Transients, tourists, and newcomers to the area lack knowledge of local hazards and the history of local disasters, so they may react differently.
- Family composition: Families, more than individuals, tend to heed evacuation warnings. Research indicates that people tend to confer with family, extended family, and friends prior to making a decision. They do this to ensure that their loved ones are safe and also to determine whether they may need to provide protection for their loved ones. Their decisions are based on the following factors related to family composition:
- Family network: People are more likely to act if they have relatives nearby who may warn them and offer them short-term shelter.
- Presence of children: Concern for children's safety will elicit quicker response from parents.
- Presence of pets: People often view their pets as they would their children and will take action to protect them. However, whereas families with children usually act more quickly to take precautions, in emergencies requiring evacuation, people with pets may endanger their own lives by refusing to evacuate, because many public shelters do not allow pets.

- Access and functional needs: Individuals with access and functional needs may need alerts in accessible formats and additional time and assistance for evacuating.

Additional Factors Influencing Public Response to a Warning

The following additional social factors also influence the extent to which warnings and alerts are received, comprehended, and heeded:

- Age: The very young and the elderly may not be able to receive and/or respond appropriately to alerts and warnings. Many in this group may also need assistance.
- Language: Non-English-speaking persons may not understand warnings that are provided in English. Communities with high percentages of non-English-speaking people should issue warnings in the primary language(s) of the population as well as in English.
- Individuals with access and functional needs: Alternative alert and warning methods are needed for individuals with access and functional needs such as the blind or low-vision and deaf or hard of hearing. Both audio and equivalent text messages should be available.
- Type of community: Residents of rural communities may have more difficulty receiving warnings than those living in urban areas.
- Level of individual preparedness: People who have taken the time to prepare for hazards (i.e., they have a plan and disaster supply kit, and have exercised the plan) are more likely to heed warning and act appropriately. Getting the preparedness buy-in is often the challenge.

Myths Associated with Public Response to Warning Messages

The following are popular myths associated with public response to warning messages:

- People usually panic in response to warnings: People DO NOT panic in response to warnings. People do not go running wildly through the streets when they hear a warning. Rather, they seek additional information to make a response decision.
- If you false alarm or "Cry Wolf" with your warnings, the public will tune you out: While there is a limit to the public's trust, "Cry Wolf" syndrome is NOT a problem IF "false alarms" are well explained and understood; people do take into account that officials are making difficult decisions to protect them from harm.
- An effective warning message is a simple one, with as little detail as possible: The 'less is more' principle does not apply for public warnings. Research has shown that people need sufficient information to validate their risk and spur them to take appropriate action.

- People usually understand what the sounding of various siren signals mean: People DO NOT always understand what the sounding of various siren signals mean. The best use of outdoor warning sirens is to alert people to immediately seek additional information about an imminent threat.

Resources

- **Applying for IPAWS Access**: *https://www.fema.gov/integrated-public-alert-warning-system* for more information on how to apply to FEMA for access to IPAWS.
- **Event Codes**: *http://www.weather.gov/os/eas_codes.shtml* for more information on event codes.
- **Planning Templates**: For more information on use of Planning Templates, *http://www.fema.gov/pdf/about/divisions/npd/CPG_101_V2.pdf*, view page 3-9 of FEMA's Comprehensive Preparedness Guide.
- **Warnings Research:** *http://orise.orau.gov/CSEPP/publications/files/CommunicationFinal.pdf* for a discussion of research findings.
- **Writing Accessible Alerts and Warning Messages**: For more information on writing accessible alerts and warning messages, *http://ncam.wgbh.org/invent_build/analog/alerts/information-requirementsalerts*.

Lesson Summary

This lesson provided an overview of creating appropriate, effective, and accessible alert and warning messages.
You should now be able to:

- Identify the basis for determining who is authorized to send IPAWS alert and warning messages
- Apply criteria for sending appropriate alert messages
- Identify the components of effective alert and warning messages
- Apply criteria for creating accessible alert and warning messages
- Describe factors that influence public response to warning messages
- Discuss the myths associated with public response to warning messages

In the next lesson, you will be introduced to the Common Alerting Protocol and various channels used for disseminating IPAWS alert and warning messages.

Lesson 3: Common Alerting Protocol Message Composition

Lesson Overview

This lesson provides an introduction to the Common Alerting Protocol (CAP), its component elements, and their associated values. It also identifies how a CMAS message is mapped from CAP.

Upon completion of this lesson, you should be able to:

- Define CAP
- Identify some of the commonly used CAP elements and their associated values
- Identify how a CMAS message is mapped from CAP

What is Common Alerting Protocol (CAP)?

The Common Alerting Protocol (CAP) is an XML-based data format standard for exchanging alert data among many different technologies and systems. CAP allows a warning message to be sent simultaneously over many CAP-compliant warning systems to many different outlets (such as radio, television, cell phones, Internet).

CAP is a well established international technical specification developed by the Organization for the Advancement of Structured Information Standards (OASIS). The concept grew out of an earlier effort of the Partnership for Public Warning.

CAP Data Elements

This lesson describes some of the commonly used data elements and their corresponding values that the alert originator either selects or composes using CAP-compliant alert authoring software. Note that your software may provide slightly different labels for these data elements:

- Urgency: Available values for the urgency element are:
    - "Immediate" - Responsive action should be taken immediately
    - "Expected" - Responsive action should be taken soon (within next hour)
    - "Future" - Responsive action should be taken in the near future
    - "Past" - Responsive action is no longer required
    - "Unknown" - Urgency not known

Only those alerts with an urgency of immediate or expected meet the requirements of the Commercial Mobile Alert System "imminent threat" alert.

- Severity: Available values for the severity element are:
    - "Extreme" - Extraordinary threat to life or property
    - "Severe" - Significant threat to life or property
    - "Moderate" - Possible threat to life or property
    - "Minor" - Minimal to no known threat to life or property
    - "Unknown" - Severity unknown

Only those alerts with a severity of extreme or severe meet the requirements of the Commercial Mobile Alert System "imminent threat" alert.

- Certainty: Available values for the certainty element are:
    - "Observed" - Determined to have occurred or to be ongoing
    - "Likely" - Probability is greater than or equal to 50%
    - "Possible" - Probability is less than 50%
    - "Unlikely" - Not expected to occur
    - "Unknown" - Certainty unknown

Only those alerts with a certainty of observed or likely meet the requirements of the Commercial Mobile Alert System "imminent threat" alert.

- Event code: Alerts intended for the Emergency Alert System, the Commercial Mobile Alert System, and/or the NWS HazCollect system must use one of the three letter codes discussed in the previous lesson. Typically, authoring software will provide a pick list of event names for the user (e.g. Civil Emergency Message) and assign the corresponding code (e.g. CEM) to the CAP alert.
- Event Category: Available values for the category element are:
    - "Geo" - Geophysical (including landslides)
    - "Met" - Meteorological (including floods)
    - "Safety" - General emergency and public safety
    - "Security" - Law enforcement, military, homeland and local/private security
    - "Rescue" - Rescue and recovery
    - "Fire" - Fire suppression and rescue
    - "Health" - Medical and public health
    - "Env" - Pollution and other environmental
    - "Transport" - Public and private transportation
    - "Infra" - Utility, telecommunication, other non-transport infrastructure
    - "CBRNE" - Chemical, Biological, Radiological, Nuclear or High-Yield Explosive threat or attack
    - "Other" - Other events

These values are used by the Commercial Mobile Alert System if the event code is missing or does not match the required event codes.

- Expires: The expires element contains a date/time value specified by the originator. For EAS, CMAS and HazCollect, all messages are deemed to be effective from the time they are sent to IPAWS. Although the expires element is optional per the CAP specification, it is a required element for all messages relayed to IPAWS for routing to these three systems.
- Headline: This is a text element defined as a "brief, human-readable headline" that is composed by the alert originator. For the NWS HazCollect system, the headline must be no longer than 160 characters including blank spaces. Internet services may use the headline value to populate Short Message Service (SMS) text, intended for subscriber-based, non-CMAS mobile systems, in which case the number of characters may be limited to 140.
- Description: This is a text element defined as "an extended human readable description of the hazard or event that occasioned this message" that is composed by the alert originator. The value of this element is not used by the Commercial Mobile Alert System, but should be used for all alerts routed to the Emergency Alert System and HazCollect. This is where you place the important information (who, what, when, and where) about the hazardous situation.
- Instruction: This text element is defined as "describing the recommended action to be taken by recipients of the alert message" that is composed by the alert originator. The value of this element is not used by the Commercial Mobile Alert System (see Response Type below), but should be used for all alerts routed to the Emergency Alert System and HazCollect. This is where you place the important information (how and why) of your protective behavior instruction. Broadcast EAS messages are limited by FCC rules to two minutes. For HazCollect, the total number of words for the description and instruction combined should not exceed 160 words, and this is a good rule of thumb for all EAS messages.
- Response Type: Available values for the response type elements that are used by the Commercial Mobile Alert System are:
    - "Shelter" - Take shelter in place or per instruction
    - "Evacuate" - Relocate as instructed in the instruction
    - "Prepare" - Make preparations per the instruction
    - "Execute" - Execute a pre-planned activity identified in instruction
    - "Avoid" - Avoid the subject event as per the instruction
    - "Monitor" - Attend to information sources as described in instruction

These values are used by IPAWS to convert to message text that is routed to CMAS.

- Area Description: The area description element is defined as a "text description of the affected area" composed by the alert originator. The value of this element is not used by the Commercial Mobile Alert System.

- Geocode: IPAWS messages intended for EAS, CMAS and/or HazCollect should contain one or more location codes, usually corresponding to the county or counties for which the alert has been issued. If you have been authorized through the application process to issue alerts for more than one county, your software may present you with a pick list of county names and assign the corresponding FIPS code to the CAP alert.
- Polygon/Circle: Your authoring software may provide a map interface that allows you to draw a polygon or circle to define the affected area of the alert message and assign corresponding values to the CAP alert. Dissemination services that include a mapping component can then retrieve and display the more precise warning area. Cellular mobile service providers may opt to use the boundaries of the geospatially defined area to activate specific cell towers.
- Resource: The optional resource element and related sub-elements offer the ability to incorporate multi-media such as images, audio, video, etc. Your authoring software may reference these files as attachments.

"Mapping" between CAP and CMAS

The primary purpose of a CMAS message is to briefly alert the recipient that a hazardous event is occurring (or will occur) in the geographic area in which the recipient is located. The CMAS specification limits the message to not more than 90 characters.

As noted in the previous section, CMAS does not use any values from the CAP description, instruction, or area description elements for "imminent threat" alerts. Instead, IPAWS generates text derived from other CAP elements to compose the message using a specific format.

- CMAS Message Format:

  "*[Event name corresponding to event code element]*

  in this area until

  [Expiration time in local time zone derived from expires element].

  [Assigned value derived from instruction-specific event code (EVI, SPW) or response type element per below].

  [Sender Name value, typically associated with the alert originator log in ID]"

- Assigned Values

  The assigned values are as follows:

- o EVI/Evacuate="Evacuate now"
- o SPW/Shelter="Take shelter now"
- o Prepare="Prepare for Action"
- o Execute="Execute Action"
- o Monitor="Monitor Radio or TV"
- o Avoid="Avoid Hazard"

CAP to CMAS Message Conversion Example

Using this format for generating a CMAS message from CAP elements, here is an example of a message converted to CMAS.

CAP Message	CMAS Message
Event Code: FFW	Flash Flood Warning
Geocode: 006109	In this area
Expires: 2003-06-17T16:00:00-07:00	until 7:00 PM PDT
Response Type: Avoid Headline: FLASH FLOOD WARNING ISSUED FOR TUOLUMNE COUNTY Description: THE NATIONAL WEATHER SERVICE IN JACKSONVILLE HAS ISSUED A * FLOOD WARNING FOR URBAN AREAS AND SMALL STREAMS IN NORTHERN TUOLUMNE COUNTY * UNTIL 700 PM PDT * AT 523 PM PDT...WEATHER SERVICE DOPPLER RADAR INDICATED AN AREA OF STRONG AND SLOW MOVING THUNDERSTORMS PRODUCING VERY HEAVY RAINFALL. THESE STORMS HAVE ALREADY PRODUCED RAINFALL ACCUMULATIONS OF 5 TO 7 INCHES...WITH ANOTHER 2 TO 4 INCHES LIKELY THROUGH 700 PM PDT THIS EVENING.	Avoid hazard.

Instruction:
PRECAUTIONARY/PREPAREDNESS
ACTIONS...

DO NOT DRIVE YOUR VEHICLE INTO
AREAS WHERE THE WATER COVERS THE
ROADWAY. THE WATER DEPTH MAY BE
TOO GREAT TO ALLOW YOUR CAR TO
CROSS SAFELY. MOVE TO HIGHER
GROUND.

Resources

- **NWS CAP 1.2 Wiki**:
  https://wiki.citizen.apps.gov/nws_developers/index.php/Category:Common_Alerti ng_Protocol.
- **OASIS CAP 1.2 Standard**: *http://www.oasis-open.org/committees/download.php/14759/emergency-CAPv1.2.pdf.*
- **NWS Warning Criteria Reference Chart**: This is a spreadsheet used by NWS listing various types of alerts with urgency, severity, and certainty. It can be accessed only as part of this course in Lesson 3.
- **Local Codes:** *http://www.census.gov/geo/www/ansi/countylookup.html*

Lesson Summary

This lesson provided an overview of the commonly used Common Alerting Protocol elements and their associated values. It also identified how a CMAS message is mapped from CAP.

You should now be able to:

- Define CAP
- Identify some of the commonly used CAP elements and their associated values
- Identify how a CMAS message is mapped from CAP